After We're Gone

After We're Gone

A Christian Perspective on Estate and
Life Planning for Families That Include
a Dependent Member with a Disability

by Duane Ruth-Heffelbower

Third edition, 2011

Library of Congress Cataloging-in-Publication Data
Ruth-Heffelbower, Duane, 1949-
    After We're Gone: a Christian Perspective on Estate and Life Planning for
Families That Include a Dependent Member with a Disability / by Duane Ruth-
Heffelbower. — 3rd ed.
      p. cm
    Includes bibliographical references.
    ISBN 978-0-8361-9565-1 (pbk. : alk. paper)
    1. Estate planning—United States—Popular works. 2. Trusts and trustees—
United States—Popular works. 3. People with disabilities—Legal status, laws,
etc.—United States—Popular works. 4. Christians—United States—Handbooks,
manuals, etc. 5. Parents of children with disabilities—United States—
Handbooks, manuals, etc. 6. Finance, Personal—Religious aspects—Christianity.
I. Title.
    KF750.Z9R88 2011
    332.024'016–dc22

                              2011004452

Third edition ©2011 by Mennonite Publishing Network, edited by Christine J.
Guth and Paul D. Leichty. This third edition is a thorough revision and update of
earlier editions. It is a companion to *Supportive Care in the Congregation*, which
describes a model of supportive care groups for persons with disabilities and their
families. Both books are available from Anabaptist Disabilities Network:
www.adnetonline.org; P.O. Box 959, Goshen, IN 46527; (574) 535-7053.

Previously published as:
    *After We're Gone: Estate and life planning for a disabled person's family: A Christian
perspective*. By Duane Ruth-Heffelbower, Mitchell L. Kingsley, and Dean A. Preheim-
Bartel. Published by Mennonite Central Committee, Mennonite Mental Health Services,
Mennonite Developmental Disability Services, 1987.

    *What happens after we're gone?: Estate and life planning for families in which a dependent
member has a disability or mental illness: Written from a Christian perspective*. By Duane
Ruth-Heffelbower. Published by Mennonite Mutual Aid, 1996.

ISBN: 978-0-8361-9565-1

Design by: Kevin Cook

Printed in the United States of America

Contents

Preface

Being responsible for the care of an adult who is dependent due to a disability of any kind is a major task. Making provisions for that person's physical, emotional, and financial well-being after the death of the caregiver can be complicated.

We note at the outset that disability in this book refers to any limiting condition, including a mental illness, that prevents a person from being financially self-supporting and/or living independently without supports.

This book illustrates the special challenges faced by dependent adults and their caregivers. It points out some of the things you need to consider when determining care for a dependent adult after you die. You will find out how you can make provisions through legal procedures and support from the faith community.

Anabaptist Disabilities Network (ADNet) is pleased to offer this thorough revision and update of these materials as the first in a series of books designed to respond to the needs of Christian families and congregations in the 21st century. We observe that the structures of modern North American society often cause people living with disabilities to be marginalized, hidden away, and excluded. The underlying premise of this book, held in common with the series as a whole, is that the faith community offers both a theological and practical foundation for ways of relating that instead support, encourage, and include persons with disabilities.

After We're Gone is one model showing how the family and faith community can interact with the legal system to make provisions for the ongoing care of persons with disabilities. The companion book, *Supportive Care in the Congregation*, addresses the faith community's interaction with the social service system as well as the fabric of the larger society surrounding the family and congregation.

I want to especially acknowledge two persons who have made this 2011 revision possible. The original author, Duane Ruth-Heffelbower, gave not only his consent but also his hearty cooperation and legal expertise for the updating of a few sections. Christine Guth, serving as a volunteer Program Associate for ADNet has given extensively of her experience and expertise in both editing and the world of disabilities. A profound thanks goes to each of them.

May we all experience a richer sense of community as we include persons with disabilities in our common life together in Jesus Christ, whose name be praised!

> Paul D. Leichty
> Executive Director
> Anabaptist Disabilities Network (ADNet)
> December 2010

Acknowledgments

Anabaptist Disabilities Network wishes to thank the following organizations for their financial support in preparing the current edition:

> Everence Financial (formerly MMA)
> Fransen Family Foundation
> Schowalter Foundation
> Jubilee Association of Maryland
> Oregon Mennonite Residential Services

1

Thinking over a life plan

Carol is in her late thirties and needs constant supervision and assistance in accomplishing basic tasks such as getting dressed. Her disability resulted from serious brain damage she experienced at birth. Carol has two brothers. Her parents are members of a Mennonite church in Oregon.

Mike is in his early thirties and reads, understands issues, and communicates at a basic level. The youngest in a family of six, Mike was born with Down Syndrome. Mike and his parents attend a Church of the Brethren congregation in Pennsylvania.

Carlos is in his late twenties. Although he successfully completed two years at a Mennonite college, he dropped out after failing several classes his junior year. A counselor referred him to a psychiatrist who diagnosed schizophrenia. Carlos is an only child. His parents are part of a Mennonite church in Texas.[1]

---

1   Stories are composite from many situations. Names and identifying details correspond to no single individual or family.

What will happen to our child after we're gone? This question plagues nearly every parent with an adult child who has a significant disability. Many state and private agencies have responded in various ways to this question, and many books and articles have been written on the subject.

Why another book? Many Christian parents are looking for an element not offered by secular agencies and foundations: the involvement of the church community. *After We're Gone* addresses life planning, wills, estates, guardianship, trusts, and related issues from a Christian perspective. It proposes involving the whole family and the family's congregation in making decisions about future caregiving, nurture, and support of dependent adults.

> *Disability in this book refers broadly to any limiting condition, including a mental illness, that prevents a person from being financially self-supporting and/or living independently without supports.*

This resource also addresses many of the questions parents raise when doing estate and life planning. It is intended to guide and encourage families in the life planning process. It does not necessarily present answers. Rather, this book points out the many considerations and options that families should think about when planning for a dependent adult family member.

After We're Gone was written as a companion resource to *Supportive Care in the Congregation*. The latter resource, available from Anabaptist Disabilities Network (ADNet), details a model for providing congregationally based supportive care groups for persons who have significant disabilities of any kind and are therefore significantly dependent. A supportive care group commits itself to long-term involvement with a person who is dependent. Readers who lack church connections may discover similar resources in their own networks of friends and family.

Through such groups, issues such as guardianship, living arrangements, trust, money management, friendship, and advocacy may be addressed. Ideally, a caring family and caring congregation will work together to ensure a secure and meaningful future for those who need significant supports in daily living.

We have taken considerable effort to present difficult technical and legal issues in understandable terms. We hope you will find this book enlightening, informative, and helpful. It is never too soon to begin planning for the future of a dependent family member.

2

Being a good steward

The earth is the Lord's and all that is in it,
the world, and those who live in it.
Psalm 24:1

Now the whole group of those who believed were of
one heart and soul, and no one claimed private owner-
ship of any possessions, but everything they owned was
held in common. There was not a needy person among
them, for as many as owned lands or houses sold them
and brought the proceeds of what was sold. They laid
it at the apostles' feet, and it was distributed to each as
any had need. Acts 4:32, 34–35

For the past ten years, Carol has been living at a group
home not far from her parents, with five other adults with
disabilities. The government provides most of Carol's living
expenses. This support includes Medicaid, Social Security,
and Supplemental Security Income benefits.

Mike lived with his parents until three years ago when he
moved into a group home in Pennsylvania. The home for
eight adults with disabilities is run by a church-related
organization. Medicare pays for a portion of Mike's living

expenses, and Mike's parents pay the remaining costs of his care.

Carlos lives semi-independently in an apartment in the basement of his parents' home. Although in the past he has held jobs for as long as a year, he has been unable to work for two years and has recently begun receiving Supplemental Security Income. When his insurance ran out, he applied for Medicaid and his application was approved.

The Bible teaches that God is the creator and owner of all things, and we have been put in charge as God's trustees. The access we have been given to material things is only as caretakers of God's trust.

As Christians, we have the responsibility to be good stewards of the resources available to us. That's why estate planning is important. It helps us to be accountable for all that we have accumulated in our lifetime—not just the portion we give to charity.

Life is transient

Because each of us is on earth for a relatively short time, and none of us knows when we're going to die, it is important that we express our intentions for the future use and disbursement of our material resources. This is especially important if we anticipate that a member of our family will always remain significantly dependent on others. The dependent family member requires extra consideration in the estate planning process.

The role of government benefits

The high cost of residential and social services makes it unrealistic for most families to anticipate that parents will have a large enough estate to cover all the needs of a dependent family member. Some kind of back-up system is needed.

Some Christians believe that support of dependent family members should be independent of government programs. They maintain that if churches today were functioning in the way that the book of Acts describes the early church, the church would be able to take care of members' needs without government assistance.

However, the high cost of specialized services needed by some persons with disabilities also strains the capacities of a typical congregation as well as organized mutual aid systems. Most Christians would thus view the larger society and the government as having an appropriate role in caring for persons who are largely dependent on others for daily living.

Indeed, most persons in the U.S. and Canada who have a significant disability are eligible for government benefits. These benefits are made possible by the assessed contributions we all make to the Social Security Administration in the U.S., the Canada Pension Plan, and other forms of taxation.

Given that reality, many Christians believe it is appropriate to structure estate planning so that dependent adults are able to remain eligible for government benefits. They believe that families and congregations need to work together with government programs to meet the needs of dependent family members. This type of specialized planning is presented later in this book. You, along with your church community, will need to decide whether accepting government benefits for your dependent child is appropriate.

The role of the church

As stewards of God's resources, we should also consider ways to support the church's work in the areas of disabilities and mental illness. For example, when establishing a trust for a family member with a disability, we may choose to consider making the final beneficiary a church agency that supports families and includes persons with disabilities in the life of the church. Consult with those agencies and/or a denominational foundation such as Mennonite Foundation for assistance.

The impetus for this book came from the dilemmas and confusion experienced by parents as they attempted to arrange their affairs so that their dependent family members would have some future security. This book responds to frequently asked questions and provides various options for consideration within the context of the Christian community.

3

Planning for the future

All people are grass,
their constancy is like the flower of the field.
The grass withers, the flower fades,
when the breath of the LORD blows upon it;
surely the people are grass.
Isaiah 40:6b–7

As Carol reached adulthood, her parents began laying out long-term plans for the future of their dependent daughter. The planning process involved receiving counsel from the director of a church-based disability advocacy organization. They read an earlier edition of this book and its companion, Supportive Care in the Congregation.

Carol's parents then met with representatives of the Mennonite church where they are members. The congregation decided to take responsibility for Carol's care in the event she survives her parents, her two brothers, and their wives. The congregation gave Carol's parents written notification to this effect.

Over the last decade, many changes have taken place in the congregation, including the appointment of a new pastor.

Many church members, including the new pastor, were not aware of the church's prior commitment to Carol's future care. The congregation is now re-evaluating their decision to serve as co-guardians for Carol. They are also considering a recommendation to form a support group to support her parents in their role as Carol's guardians.

Carlos's parents find it difficult to know what the future will hold for their son. Although he is currently in need of government benefits, they continue to hope that treatment will stabilize his mental health and that he can eventually support himself. Yet they accept that responsible planning for his future must allow for the possibility of relapse or little improvement in his condition. Although his parents are active in their church congregation, Carlos himself rarely attends.

Most of us try to live our lives to the fullest. But it is prudent that we make provisions for individuals who are dependent on us so they will be provided for after we die. This is especially significant if you are the parent of an adult child who needs support in many aspects of daily life. For such situations, life planning is particularly important. Life planning means putting plans in place to provide for your dependents, including your adult child with a long-term disabling condition.

Involve your family, friends, church

As the parent of a dependent adult, it is natural that you are concerned about your child's long-term well-being and future financial and emotional security. Because unique considerations are involved, it is especially important to include members of your family, circle of friends and congregation in the life planning decisions. It is important to include in planning anyone who is likely to carry any long-term responsibility for the person with the disability. Think creatively about who else might welcome the invitation to be a long-term friend and support to your family member. Life planning does well to include the following people:

The dependent person

Though it may not be appropriate in every situation, it is generally best to include the dependent person to the extent he or she is able to be involved. If the dependent person has a guardian or conservator, that person will need to be included as well.

Siblings

Estate and life planning should be a family process. This helps facilitate the open expression of opinions and feelings about future expectations. Sibling participation in planning also helps avoid surprises for the brothers and sisters concerning plans for their dependent sibling after the death of their parents. Thoughtful and sensitive planning by parents will not only discourage disputes after their death, but in many cases, it might become a final and enduring expression of their love. In spite of—and perhaps because of—our reluctance to talk about death, life planning is an important activity for the whole family.

Extended family

Sometimes the emotional or geographical closeness of extended family members (uncles, aunts, cousins, etc.) makes it important to include them in the life planning process. In some cases, they may carry specific roles in the future, as they help to maintain and care for the dependent family member.

Friends

In our increasingly mobile society, many rely on friends for roles that family played in earlier generations. Consider who among your circle of friends and acquaintances has taken a special interest in your dependent family member. Who has interests in common with your child and has an open and generous heart? Recognize that the invitation to be a long-term friend and support to your family member is an opportunity for connection that will benefit both parties in the friendship.

Your church

If members of your church play a significant role in the life of your dependent adult, it would be beneficial to include them in the life planning process. The church has a responsibility to ensure that the dependent person has lifetime emotional and spiritual support and care. This is part of our mutual accountability as members of the body of Christ.

Issues to consider

Here are issues you need to consider when you begin an estate and life planning process:

- Do an appraisal of how your family functions and who typically performs various roles. Future responsibilities with regard to the estate and care of your dependent family member should not be given or accepted only out of obligation. Rather, they should be given and accepted in response to peoples' personal commitments and abilities.
- Review the capabilities and resources of your dependent family member and determine what kind of support and assistance he or she will need in the future. When possible, identify your dependent family member's wishes and desires for the future in terms of work, living arrangements, church involvement, etc.
- Determine what kinds of living arrangements the dependent adult family member will most likely need after the parents' death. Find out how estate planning can be done now to help facilitate those options later. Determine who will ensure that an appropriate living arrangement is secured when needed.
- Take stock of the financial, emotional, and human resources available to develop and implement a life plan.

Resources to consider in life planning

Financial resources

What assets will be available when you are no longer alive? Will the assets be available as ready cash or tied up in long-term investments such as stocks, bonds, or real estate? What kind of financial management will be required to adequately care for these assets?

If you do not have a large legacy to pass on to your dependent adult child, you need to ask important questions. How much of your assets will you be able to pass on? Should you use a life insurance policy to fund a trust for your dependent child?

As you can see, planning in this area will need to address the person's particular needs. Subsequent sections of this book will describe useful tools regarding finances.

Family and friends

How can family and friends help fill the needs of your dependent adult family member? Are brothers and sisters available to assist a dependent sibling? Do they live close to their sibling, and are they likely to continue to live nearby?

Because of the extensive needs of some persons with disabilities and the substantial commitment required to take on care that a parent has been providing, sensitivity is critical here. This may be especially true when the disability is a mental illness. Brothers or sisters may not feel able to accept all or any of the responsibility for their dependent sibling. Parents of a person with a disability may intentionally or unintentionally generate guilt among their other children who are unable to accept such responsibility.

Friends and extended family members may also serve as valuable resources in meeting future needs. Some families find friends who are willing to take an active role through support groups of various kinds. It is important to involve everyone in planning who is likely to be involved in care later.

Spiritual and church resources

Siblings or other family members may find the care of a dependent brother or sister an overwhelming prospect because of the great demands and lifelong potential. However, the church is uniquely suited to lessen that burden, or to play a primary role when no family members are available. A premise of this book is that the church community is an important resource to persons living with disabilities of all kinds, including mental illness.

The church has the spiritual and human resources to be a friend, advocate, and guardian of such persons. The book, *Supportive Care in the Congregation*, describes a model for providing a caring network of people around dependent persons. After a dependent person's parents have passed away, the human and spiritual resources available from the church can make the difference between living in isolation and being part of a loving, caring community. Therefore, discovering and developing these resources are important aspects of life planning.

Finding help to do life planning

A variety of people can offer needed expertise and counsel. Estate and life planning counselors from your congregation, denomination, or other church agency can help to bring a Christian perspective to this process. Representatives from a church disability office or denominational foundation may also be able to provide valuable advice.

An attorney (lawyer) should serve as the technical adviser for setting up the documents of an estate and life plan. Look for an attorney who has knowledge about the unique considerations of families of persons with disabilities. Attorneys may appreciate your introducing them to available resources on the subject. Offer your attorney this book to help him or her in advising you.

Taking the next step

Planning will involve writing a will and, in many cases, creating a trust. You may also choose to create a guardianship or nominate a conservator. In most cases, planning will also entail setting up informal friend and advocacy relationships through your local congregation on behalf of your family member with a disability.

The purpose of such planning is to make adequate resources available to the person with a disability and to preserve his or her rights and freedoms. The objective is to help the individual grow to his or her full capacity.

4

Preparing a will

For everything there is a season,
and a time for every matter under heaven:
a time to be born, and a time to die.
Ecclesiastes 3:1–2a

Carol is unable to manage her own affairs and might lose government benefits if she were given a sizable estate. As a result, Carol's parents have not included Carol in their will. However, they have placed a letter of intent with their will, setting forth expectations for Carol's ongoing personal and medical care, including provisions for her burial.

Mike is also unable to manage his own affairs. However, his parents have chosen to name Mike in their will. They have decided to establish a trust in which proceeds from their estate will be placed. This will enable Mike to receive periodic payments from the estate without losing his government benefits. Mike's parents have also placed funds in the bank account of Mike's sister, with the understanding that the money will be used for Mike's care after their deaths.

Carlos's parents have amended their wills so that Carlos is not named directly. Like Mike's parents, they have established a trust that will receive the assets from their estate. Carlos's grandparents have also designated this trust to receive assets from their estate on Carlos's behalf.

A will is a legal instrument that allows people to direct how their assets will be invested and distributed after their deaths. If you die without leaving a will, the law provides that your property will be passed on to your nearest relatives, typically to a spouse and children, or if none are surviving, to other close relatives, such as parents.

If both parents of a dependent person die without leaving a will, that person ordinarily would receive his or her share outright. An outright gift to some persons with disabilities may not be advisable. For this reason, it is especially important for parents of adults with such disabilities to make a will.

Purpose of a will

A will makes it possible for you to dispose of property of any kind and designate the recipients. A trust can be part of your will. As the parent of a person with a disability, you can name the people who will become trustees to invest and distribute funds for your dependent child.

Creating a will

To create a will, begin by taking account of the assets and debts that would be left in your estate. After reading this book, talk with an adviser about the options for planning for the future in order to provide for your dependent family member. Then, talk with your family about the decisions you will need to make concerning your estate.

Next, go to your attorney. Take along a list of your assets, your ideas about possible options for making provision for your dependent family member, your questions, and this book. Your attorney should be able to help clarify your ideas by asking further questions and informing you of relevant laws of your state or province. Your attorney may have to conduct further research based on your suggestions or issues raised in this book. Ask your attorney about fees at the first meeting so there is no misunderstanding. Wills are not expensive, but not having one can be.

Benefits and inheritance

Consider what financial resources and benefits are available for your dependent family member. In the U.S., the most common government benefits available to persons with disabilities are Social Security, Supplemental Security Income (SSI), Medicare, and Medicaid. Let's examine each of these benefits briefly.

Social Security

Benefits are available through Social Security because a parent or the person with a disability has paid into the system, usually via their employee wages. These benefits may be available to the dependent person under two circumstances: a) upon the parents' retirement, death, or disability, if the child was born with or acquired a disability before age 22, or b) because of the dependent person's own contribution to the system through employment.

Supplemental Security Income

Stringent eligibility criteria are involved in receiving SSI benefits (administered by Social Security). To be eligible for benefits, individuals must show proof of disability and be unable to hold gainful employment. Strict income and financial resource limitations also apply.

Both earned and unearned income will be counted in determining eligibility for SSI. The parents' income is considered if the child is age 18 or under (or until age 21 if the child is a student).

An individual may have some cash resources and still qualify for SSI. Small amounts of earned income may also be permissible. Check with your Social Security office for eligibility criteria.

Medicare and Medicaid

Once an adult qualifies for SSI, he or she usually qualifies for other local, state, and federal benefits, such as medical assistance (Medicaid), rehabilitation training, housing, social, and supportive services. Under some conditions, adults with disabilities under the age of 65 may also be eligible for Medicare.

Options to consider

Any taxpayer and contributor to the Social Security system has the right to obtain benefits for a dependent family member. An objective of the specialized estate planning we are advocating in this book is to maintain a dependent person's eligibility for government benefits and services while using your estate to supplement these benefits.

Typically, government benefits do not cover all needs of an individual. Therefore, parents usually desire to make some financial resources available to enhance the well-being of their dependent family member. In preparing their will, parents may seek to provide for their dependent member's financial future without jeopardizing government benefits. Here are some options from which you may choose:

- You can make a direct bequest to your child as you would to any other beneficiary. However, this may disqualify your child from entitlement to most government benefits until the bequest is spent down to required limits. Therefore, unless the bequest will be sizable enough to provide lifetime care, this is the least desirable option. Also, persons with developmental disabilities or certain forms of mental illness may have considerable difficulty managing money, especially sizable amounts.

- You can disinherit your dependent child, resulting in him or her becoming entirely dependent on government benefits and private donations, or upon earnings, if possible. In so doing, you may choose to leave your dependent child's portion to a sibling or other close relative with the suggestion that the assets be used for the dependent person's needs. This option may be chosen when family members have a close relationship with this individual and are capable and willing to share the inheritance. Regardless of the parents' wishes, however, the family member controlling the assets is not legally obligated to use the funds for the person who has a disability. This arrangement is appealing in its simplicity and in the fact that it eases the difficulty of obtaining government benefits. Check with your attorney concerning any written instructions you give to make sure they don't modify the will.

- A discretionary trust could be funded with assets from your estate. The funds in the discretionary trust would supplement governmental benefits that may be available for your dependent child. The trust could be included in your will as a testamentary trust. It could also be made effective immediately as a living trust that you could revoke or change. The discretionary trust is described in detail in the next chapter.

- You can purchase an insurance policy on the life of someone who is currently providing significant financial support and create a discretionary trust to hold insurance proceeds for the dependent family member. This is the quickest and least expensive way to create an estate if few other financial resources exist. Obtain advice from a knowledgeable insurance agent as well as an attorney.

Naming an executor

In your will, you should name whomever you wish to carry out the instructions of your will. This executor (sometimes called a personal representative), subject to the probate court, will carry out the terms of your will. Ordinarily, many minor and administrative decisions will be made in consultation with the beneficiaries. Under the laws of some states and provinces, where the value of the estate is under a certain amount, the executor can proceed without court approval.

Final instructions

You may desire to leave more detailed instructions or wishes than are appropriate in the will. This can be done with an informal document called a "letter of intent" or "letter of last instructions." This non-binding document may describe in detail what you feel will be best for your dependent son or daughter in the future. It may also describe some of the unique needs and wishes of, or pertaining to, your dependent son or daughter that only you may be aware of. The letter could also detail your wishes concerning your own funeral and burial. Check this document with your attorney to avoid having it modify your will.

An executor needs freedom to deal with changes in circumstances. The will along with the letter of intent can give this needed flexibility. Then, an executor, while not legally bound by such a letter, can act in ways that are consistent with your wishes.

Maintaining and changing your will

You should keep your original will with its attachments in a secure place. Tell the person named as executor where the will is located. Your attorney will also keep a copy. You can change your will at any time in consultation with an attorney. Make sure to review your will every few years to ensure that its provisions remain satisfactory.

5

Establishing a trust

*How does God's love abide in anyone who has the
world's goods and sees a brother or sister in need and
yet refuses help? Little children, let us love, not in word
or speech, but in truth and action.*
I John 3:17–18

*Mike's parents have chosen to establish a trust for him. The
parents have potential trustees in mind. One or more of
their other children have been assisting them in their roles
as caregivers.*

*Carlos's parents believe that establishing a trust for him is a
prudent option that will enable him to retain any benefits
he might be receiving at the time of their death. Carlos has
no siblings who can serve as potential trustees. Although his
relationship with many extended family members has been
strained by his illness, one of his cousins has agreed to serve
as trustee.*

A trust is one of the most important life planning tools available.
Because of its flexibility, a trust can address many different life
circumstances. Unlike an informal recommendation, a trustee
must follow your wishes. Best of all, trusts can meet the special
needs of a dependent adult.

What is meant by a trust

A trust comes into existence when one person, the trustor (also called settlor or testator), transfers money or other property to someone else (the trustee) to hold and manage for the benefit of a third person (the beneficiary). Trusts are created in wills or in separate trust agreements.

Trusts are typically used in estate planning to limit taxes and to provide management of property for a beneficiary. A trust creates a legal obligation to use trust resources as stated in the trust document.

Trusts can be established and operated during the trustor's life. In these cases, they are called living trusts. Trusts can be created in a will to take effect after the trustor's death, in which case they are called testamentary trusts.

A living trust can be revocable, in which case the trustor can change or cancel it. It can also be irrevocable, in which case the trustor cannot change it.

A trust created in a will does not take effect until death. It can be changed at any time prior to death if the trustor is competent to make a new will.

Advantages of a trust

There are many advantages to establishing a trust for a dependent adult family member. Here are some of them:

- A trust gives you the ability to provide instructions for managing and spending the property of the trust on behalf of your family member with a disability. As is described below, you can limit payouts in such a way as to preserve the eligibility of your dependent adult son or daughter for government assistance. No other method allows this to be done while control is retained over spending decisions. It is also possible to put funds in the trust before you die so that the trustee can have an opportunity to manage the property and make spending decisions under your supervision.

- Regular court supervision is generally not needed for a trust when the trust document is properly drawn up.
- You can make additions to a trust. For example, the trust can be the beneficiary of a life insurance policy on the trustor's life. Other family members can also contribute funds to the trust, and churches or other organizations can add to the fund without having to set up an entire management system.
- When the beneficiary dies, unused funds in a trust can be distributed to any person or organization. Unused funds may be designated for another family member or used to support your church or other charity.

Disadvantages of a trust

If you're thinking about establishing a trust, you probably should consider the following disadvantages:

- Some people have trouble finding a trustee in whom they can place full confidence. To eliminate this prospect, it may be useful to appoint two co-trustees or have a financial institution be co-trustee.
- Some states allow trustors to call for regular court supervision if that is desired. This involves significant costs in legal and accounting fees.
- Trustees are usually paid, although a family member or church-appointed trustee may not accept payment. You should expect the trustee to receive one-half to three-fourths of 1 percent of the amount in the trust each year as a fee. Attorney and accounting fees are additional.
- In some jurisdictions, a trust may need to pay income tax just as individuals do. Check with an attorney about local laws in your area.

Naming a beneficiary for unused trust funds

Give careful consideration to the implications of naming siblings as beneficiaries for funds in a trust after the death of your adult child with a disability, especially if the siblings are also named as trustee(s). The siblings may be deceased by the time the trust goes into effect, and their status as beneficiaries could create a potential conflict of interest. Siblings should not be inhibited from wanting to see the money spent on their dependent brother or sister. In Canada, the "even handed rule" obligates the trustee to maintain the integrity of the trust for both the current and final beneficiary.

You may consider choosing a charitable beneficiary such as an organization working for the benefit of persons with disabilities. Entities such as Christian organizations providing housing and/or support services to persons with mental illness or other disabilities would benefit from such funds in their ministry to churches and families.

Finding a trustee

Finding the right trustee can be difficult. Corporate trustees such as banks or trust companies may not be willing to exercise the kind of discretion that is critical for a dependent adult.

An individual who cares about the beneficiary is essential to the process. Trust companies and various foundations may be willing to act as co-trustees with an individual named by the parents. In this case the individual trustee makes decisions about the person's living conditions while the trust company or foundation (co-trustee) makes investment and management decisions. You may want to consider a foundation run by a Christian denomination you trust that will make investment decisions reflecting your values.

Trustees need to be replaced as they die, move away, or otherwise become unable to continue the work. This problem is the same in the case of a guardianship. Practically speaking, a trustor should name several successor trustees. The difficulty is that the trustor is usually a parent of the beneficiary, so it is most likely that the dependent person will live for many years after the trustor dies. This means many of the persons known and trusted by the trustor are also likely to die before the beneficiary.

One potential method of optimizing continuity of care after the death of parents is by designating a support group to provide successor trustees, guardians, executors, and conservators as needed. Working along with a congregation, the support group can transform the trustee function by surrounding the trustee and beneficiary with support, making the trustee's job much lighter. Such a program is described in the companion book to this guide, *Supportive Care in the Congregation.*

The discretionary spendthrift trust

Dependent people frequently receive various kinds of government aid, including health care, special education, equipment, and living expense benefits. As families with dependent members begin estate planning, they often need to ask difficult questions such as:

- Should they give the dependent child the same share of their estate as the other children? If they do so, the dependent child runs the risk of losing government benefits until the inherited funds are diminished.
- Should they disinherit their dependent child?
- Should they leave the dependent child the entire estate in hopes that it will last through their lifetime?

Many families have found the discretionary spendthrift trust to be the answer to this dilemma. A discretionary spendthrift trust is a fund set up on behalf of the dependent person to provide for special needs that are not furnished by government benefits. The dependent child's portion of the parents' estate can be placed into the discretionary trust, and parents can make additional gifts as they see fit.

Discretionary trusts keep the trust estate out of the hands of the beneficiary, giving the beneficiary periodic payments or paying for certain types of expenses. With a discretionary trust, the trustee is given absolute discretion to decide whether to give the beneficiary anything. This means no one can make the trustee pay.

Because discretionary trusts continue after parents of dependent adults pass away, attorneys who work with the families of dependent persons often use the discretionary spend-thrift trust. Legislation and court cases continue to honor such arrangements when handled properly. In Canada, discretionary trusts may include a non-vesting clause.

How large should a discretionary trust be? One rule of thumb is that the trust earnings should be consistent with the amount parents currently spend on the special needs of the family member with a disability.

The discretionary trust is the best means yet devised of managing a fund for special needs and expenses of a dependent person without making the person ineligible for government benefits. Such trusts have been used and accepted since the 1980s.

Government intrusion into discretionary trusts

For a person with a disability, the use of a discretionary trust means the government, in many jurisdictions, cannot count the trust assets when determining qualifications for government benefits. In most places it also means that the trust is not part of the estate of the person with a disability, since it passes to another beneficiary on the person's death. While many states and most Canadian provinces seem to respect them, your attorney will need to determine whether laws in your area will support and protect such a trust. As of 2009, twenty-three states had adopted the Uniform Trust Code, which respects spendthrift clauses and protects the trusts described in this book.

Some government agencies, however, have attempted to count these discretionary trusts as assets of the dependent person. This happens most dramatically in Minnesota. Minnesota law specifically disallows the use of the trust described in this book, then codifies an almost identical plan and declares its support for supplementary needs trusts.[1] It is critical for the attorney drafting one of these trusts to understand the local requirements. Be aware that few attorneys know these peculiar statutes, and you must ask about them. Give this book to your attorney.

The goal of proper drafting of a trust is to ensure that a dependent person may still qualify for government benefits. Typical trust provisions may, for example, allow the trustee to pay out for subsistence items such as food, shelter, and clothing. However, under these special circumstances, such an allowance means the trust assets are counted by the government in the same way as other resources of the beneficiary.

Therefore, it is very important that the trustee be given absolute discretion in making payments to supplement, not supplant, government benefits. If this is not done, the government may simply deny government benefits if government officials believe the trust disqualifies the person.

This is a changing area of the law, and you must have an attorney make a fresh determination of your local situation. An attorney who is willing but inexperienced in these matters should obtain assistance before attempting to draft one of these trusts. The examples provided in the back of this book are illustrative samples that should not be used without local research. A denominational foundation or disabilities office should be able to steer you to local assistance, as can secular disabilities

---

1   Minnesota Statutes 501B.89

advocacy organizations in your state or province, such as those listed in Chapter 11 of this book.

Protecting the discretionary trust

The "poison pill" clause, also called a "self-destruct" clause, is one method of thwarting attempts by the government to view discretionary trusts as assets. The poison pill provision allows the trustee to distribute all of the funds of the trust to a charity in the event a government agency attempts to require spend down of the trust before eligibility for benefits is established. When the funds are distributed, the trust "dies"—hence the name "poison pill." This action makes it less vulnerable to a government agency.

The chief drawback of such a plan is that the funds are gone forever and cannot be reclaimed when the danger is past. Another problem may arise if a government agency decides to withhold benefits on the basis of assets that are no longer available. Your attorney will need to check the local situation and advise you on this course of action. Minnesota statutes specifically disallow the poison pill provision. Other states may too. Some provinces allow trusts of a limited size to be part of a dependent person's assets without jeopardizing eligibility for government benefits.

Pooled trusts

The assets of special needs trusts are usually small compared to other types of trusts. The problem posed by small asset trusts is that there is no profit in managing them, making it difficult to find a trustee to care for the assets. If the assets are all cash, an interest-bearing bank account handled by a volunteer trustee may be adequate. Assets that require more active management, or cash the trustor hopes will grow rapidly, require a different type of trustee.

The pooled trust is a simple idea. A trustee creates a single fund, and trustors can add to the fund rather than setting up their own management scheme. This method also allows several different funds with different investment goals. Parents of a young child may want to build the trust over time and have the money professionally managed for growth. Others may want conservative management that minimizes risk for their older child.

Pooled special needs trusts are available in some locales. Arc of Indiana is a leader in this movement. Those who work with special needs trusts in your area will know what is available.

6

Setting up a guardianship

The LORD will keep you from all evil;
he will keep your life.
The LORD will keep your going out and your coming in
from this time on and forevermore.
Psalm 121:7–8

Carol's parents secured full guardianship for their dependent daughter, Carol, when she was eighteen years old. They now work with the personnel at the group home where Carol lives to ensure that her needs are met. Her parents bring Carol home once a week. This gives opportunity for Carol's parents and her brother who lives close by to visit with her. Carol's other brother, who lives in California, sees her less frequently.

Mike's parents obtained full guardianship for their dependent son Mike when he was twenty-seven. They now believe it would have been better to establish guardianship soon after he turned eighteen. Mike lives in a group home during the week and spends weekends in his parents' home. On weekends, he accompanies his parents wherever they go, including to church each Sunday. Mike is accepted as a regular part of family life and interacts freely with his brothers and sisters, and his nieces and nephews.

> *Carlos's parents have chosen not to obtain guardianship because most of the time Carlos is competent to manage his own affairs, with limited assistance. They believe he would oppose guardianship, and they do not want to evoke the adversarial relationship that might result if they tried to have him declared legally incompetent. The community mental health center serves as representative payee for his Social Security check and helps Carlos manage his money. His parents' church has formed a supportive care group[1] that supports Carlos by cleaning his apartment once a month, providing rides to appointments, and providing occasional meals and social outings.*

While God is our ultimate defender and caretaker, God has also given us the responsibility to care for one another. This area of stewardship is especially applicable to caring for others who are unable to provide for themselves. Appointing a guardian for an adult child with a long-term disability or mental illness is one example of this type of stewardship.

The meaning of guardianship

Guardianship is a legal relationship between two people. One person, called a guardian (sometimes called conservator or committee), is given the power and duty to take responsibility for making decisions for the other person who is unable to tend to his or her own affairs.

Parents are generally considered the natural guardians of their minor children. However, when a child reaches the age of eighteen, only the court can determine that an individual needs a guardian and make such an appointment. This includes adult

---

1   See the companion book, *Supportive Care in the Congregation*, available from Anabaptist Disabilities Network, P.O. Box 959, Goshen, IN 46527; (574) 535-7053, www.adnetonline.org.

children who remain dependent on their parents.

There are two types of guardianship: guardianship of the person and guardianship of the estate. Guardianship of the person gives the guardian control over the personal supervision and decision-making of the dependent person. Guardianship of the estate gives the guardian control over property and cash assets of the dependent person. The guardian is able to use those resources for the dependent person's benefit.

The same individual may act as guardian of the person and guardian of the estate. However, it is often advisable that different persons serve in these roles because of the different skills required.

When guardians are needed

You need to consider many issues before appointing a guardian for a dependent adult over age eighteen. Appointing a guardian is generally considered an action of last resort and should not be done until all other options for protecting the person have been exhausted. For alternatives, see sections below on limited guardianship and alternatives to guardianship.

Legal guardianship may not be needed by most persons with disabilities. The imposition of guardianship can severely limit the freedom of the person under the guise of providing protection. This is because it usually involves the removal of some or all of the dependent person's civil rights. In legal effect, the adult becomes a child once again.

When considering guardianship for your dependent child over age eighteen, review the following criteria before proceeding with legal action.

Consider guardianship if your dependent…

- is significantly disabled due to mental illness, dementia, intellectual disability ("mental retardation"), or other developmental disability to the point where he or she is unable to manage his or her own affairs

- is unable to care for himself or herself to the degree that harm will likely occur
- is unable to make informed decisions about proposed care, supervision, and treatment
- resides in a setting that provides for all physical needs
- will directly acquire or inherit property which he or she lacks the capacity to manage
- is refused a service without authorization by a guardian. For example, doctors and hospitals require "informed consent" before providing medical service. Without such consent, many hospitals and doctors, for fear of malpractice claims, may refuse needed services if the patient exhibits only limited understanding.
- is able to benefit substantially from a guardian's services

The presence of disability alone is not sufficient cause to seek appointment of a guardian. Education and personal skill training for a person with a disability can reduce or eliminate the need for legal guardianship. The availability of friends, family members, and advocates reduces the need even more. Perhaps most importantly, the love and care of a community of faith can provide the protection and assistance persons with limiting conditions need and desire.

Without guardianship or other legal authority, however, decisions cannot be legally made for another adult. Setting up a trust for the benefit of a dependent person provides for decision making on financial matters and may make guardianship unnecessary in some cases.

How guardianships are established

Application to the court for appointment of a guardian can be initiated by parents, siblings, friends, social agencies, or even state or provincial authorities, if the need for guardianship becomes apparent and the issues are not being dealt with by the appropriate people.

While procedures may vary depending on state or provincial law and local practice, the following steps represent the general procedure for setting up guardianship:

1. If parents or others have determined that guardianship is needed, a petition for appointment of a guardian must be filed in the proper court where the dependent person lives. A doctor's examination and recommendation for appointment of a guardian must be documented in the papers filed with the court.

2. Upon receipt of the petition, the court should appoint someone to temporarily represent the rights and best interests of the dependent person in the guardianship proceedings. This person is called a "guardian ad litem." He or she is obligated to make an independent evaluation and report to the court. This person need not be an attorney but should be an individual with understanding of persons with disabilities or other limiting conditions.

3. A date for a hearing before the court will be set. On that date, the person with the disability should appear in court along with the parents and others closely involved in the process. Ordinarily this hearing is not open to the public. The court may request testimony from professionals, parents, and the dependent person. The judge will consider all the evidence in the documents which have been filed or provided by witnesses and decide whether to appoint a guardian for the person.

4. If the court finds the person to be totally incapable of caring for his or her own needs, the court will declare the person incompetent and appoint a guardian of the person or a guardian of the estate, or both.

Limited guardianship is permitted in some states or provinces. In such cases, a guardian is appointed to take responsibility only in those areas in which the person cannot act, thus preserving all other rights.

Because there are various technicalities and safeguards surrounding the hearing process, it is usually wise to obtain the help of an attorney.

Rights of the dependent person under total guardianship

Total guardianship, also known as plenary guardianship, removes virtually all rights of the person who has been declared incompetent and gives extensive powers to the guardian. Under these conditions, some of the rights the dependent person might lose include the right to marry, make a contract, consent to surgery, or give legal consent on other matters. Additionally, the dependent person may not be able to choose a residence, education, training, or employment, obtain a driver's license, buy or sell real estate or personal property, or make a valid will. In most jurisdictions, a dependent person within a total guardianship may not vote.

The decision to appoint a plenary guardian is a very serious one, and parents should thoroughly review all other options before pursuing it.

Choosing a guardian

The court may appoint as guardian any person eighteen years of age or older who consents to act as guardian. The court must be satisfied that the guardian will act in the best interests of the dependent adult and will not have interests that conflict with those of dependent adult. For example, it would generally be unwise to have a final beneficiary serve as guardian of the dependent person's estate because of possible conflict of interest.

Parents would usually be chosen first to be a guardian. After the parents, the court should consider interested relatives and friends. The original petition to the court should identify whom the petitioners desire as guardian.

In instances where no family members are available or where they are judged inappropriate for appointment, any interested individual who meets the criteria may make application to be appointed as a guardian. This presents a unique opportunity for the dependent person's community of faith to identify an individual to serve in that capacity, as is described in the book, *Supportive Care in the Congregation.*

In their will, parents can appoint guardians and successor guardians for a minor child. However, if the dependent person is over eighteen years old and has not been declared in need of a guardian, parents may still nominate a guardian and successor guardians in their will, in the event one is needed in the future. After the parents' deaths, the nominee may petition the court and ask that the adult child be found in need of a guardian.

If parents have already been appointed guardians by the court, they may name a successor guardian in their will to assume, upon their deaths, the same powers and duties originally granted to them by the court. The court may honor parents' wishes in the appointment of a guardian. In some areas, successor guardians named in a will are not recognized.

Where no family member or private individual will undertake guardianship for a dependent adult, a public guardian may apply to the court to become that person's guardian. In Canada, the option of a public guardian is generally not available.

Several states and provinces have laws that allow for collective or corporate guardianship. In these cases, if the court determines that a guardian is needed, an agency or organization such as a local congregation could be appointed guardian if that is the best option available. The congregation in turn would delegate responsibility to one or two individuals within the congregation.

Types of guardianships

Generally, the guardian accepts responsibility to look out for the best interests of the dependent person in such a way as to encourage this adult to become as independent as possible. The guardian assists the dependent person in a variety of ways and makes decisions for him or her. The areas of responsibility and types of decisions depend on the needs and capabilities of the dependent person and the kind of guardianship. Several different types of guardianship exist.

Full or plenary guardianship

Where a court has found a person to be without any capacity to manage his or her affairs, it will appoint a full guardian (guardian of the estate and guardian of the person). A full guardian makes virtually all the important decisions for the dependent person. In effect, the dependent person has no legal rights. The guardian, however, should be committed to serving and helping that individual. The guardian may allow the dependent person to make decisions where he or she is capable of doing so. It is important to weigh carefully the effect plenary guardianship may have on the development of a person with a disability.

Limited guardianship

Limited guardianship is available in some states and provinces and is ordered by the court to cover only those areas where the person is incapable of exercising his or her rights to make some decisions. For example, limited guardianship might cover only the living arrangements or day program of a person with a disability, recognizing that the person could adequately handle the other decisions of life. A limited guardian can make decisions for the dependent person only to the extent specified in the court order covering the guardianship.

One concern raised about limited guardianship is the potential for the attitude of the guardian to limit the autonomy of the dependent person more than the legal status permits. For example, some financial institutions deal with limited guardians who have difficulty understanding the extent and limitations of their powers.

If the dependent person's conditions change or turn out to be other than first thought, the guardian may need to go back into court repeatedly for adjustment of powers. Often this type of guardianship order is time-limited and may have to be renewed by the court every several years, should circumstances warrant. It is difficult or impossible to know ahead of time exactly what powers the guardian will need or should have.

Despite the potential difficulties, limited guardianship still is one of the most significant developments in the field because it allows a less restrictive form of protection for people with disabilities. Have your attorney check the laws of your state or province to see if this option is available.

Guardian of the estate

Guardian of the estate, called conservatorship or committee in some jurisdictions, is appropriate for persons who are capable of managing their personal daily lives but are incapable of handling business or financial affairs. The guardian of the estate is required to act in place of the dependent individual in all transactions dealing with management of his or her property and income. This guardian is to ensure that the individual's income and resources are used for his or her benefit and needs to be accountable to the court regularly for all investments and expenditures.

Such a guardianship is usually created when the dependent person has substantial money and/or property. Under this arrangement, the dependent person maintains legal title to all his or her possessions. An alternative under similar circumstances is the trust, which costs less to set up and does not require court supervision.

Guardian of the person

The guardian of the person is concerned about the personal decisions and affairs of the dependent person. Powers granted by the court to a guardian of the person may include determining place of residence, controlling the dependent person's programs, or giving consent for medical and other professional care, counsel, and treatment.

Temporary guardian

A temporary guardian may be appointed by the court for a specific situation and for a short period. The most common need for a temporary guardian arises when surgery or other major medical treatment becomes necessary.

Public guardian/trustee

In some jurisdictions, the court may appoint a public guardian and/or trustee to serve dependent persons for whom no one else is available to serve as guardian. The public guardian is charged with looking after the personal needs of dependent adults.

Corporate guardianship

Corporate guardianship is guardianship provided by public agencies or non-profit organizations such as a church. Organizations have been created for the purpose of providing corporate guardianship. Families in essence purchase from an organization lifetime commitment to the dependent family member. A staff person then provides the usual guardian functions. Where permitted by law, the family may ask their local congregation to serve as guardian, thus providing personal lifetime interest in the dependent family member.

The above types of guardianships sometimes overlap. Except for temporary guardianship, all other types mentioned are considered permanent, with occasional exceptions. Guardianship can be terminated if the court decides the dependent person has gained competency.

Some states and provinces have put legal limits on the decisions any guardian can make for the dependent person. For example, in California and Kansas, a plenary guardian cannot commit the dependent person to an institution, have the person sterilized, or authorize the use of psychosurgery or experimental drugs without special court order or the consent of the dependent person. Other states and provinces have various limitations on these same matters. Courts have often imposed limits where legislation has not specifically stated them.

Alternatives to guardianship

Alternatives to guardianship may be less restrictive and still give dependent adults adequate support and direction while encouraging self-sufficiency. A sibling, other relative, or friend might agree to take responsibility for the person needing assistance. A person serving as an advocate could ensure that the dependent person's needs are met.

Congregational supportive care

Churches are encouraged to take an active role in supporting families with a dependent member as part of their responsibility as members of the family of God. The book, *Supportive Care in the Congregation*, describes how a small supportive care group can be formed to assist a dependent family member. This long-term relationship can provide continuity of care as well as many of the usual guardianship functions on an informal basis. Even if a guardian has been appointed from within the family or the congregation, we encourage that such a person be part of a support group.

Power of Attorney

A competent person can appoint someone to act as his or her agent. This agent is called an attorney in fact, and the one who gives the agent authority is called the principal. The document that gives them this authority is called power of attorney. This power can be general or specific. A general power of attorney gives the agent all the authority the principal has. A special power of attorney can list exactly what things the agent can do. These powers end when the principal dies or becomes incompetent.

A durable power of attorney for health care can appoint an agent to make decisions about the principal's health care even after the principal becomes incompetent. Durable powers of attorney for health care are established by local law and vary from place to place. Generally speaking, every competent person should give a durable power of attorney for health care to a trusted person. Durable power of attorney is particularly applicable for persons with degenerative disabilities or persons who want their affairs to be handled should they become incompetent.

Self-management

Under some circumstances, a person may foresee that he or she will need the help of a guardian in the future. This could occur, for example, in the case of a person with a degenerative disease. Such a person can nominate another individual to be his or her guardian. When the need for such help becomes apparent, the individual so nominated can petition the court to have a hearing to declare the nominator incompetent and to be appointed that person's guardian.

7

Glossary

Agent. The person named by another person to act on his or her behalf as in a power of attorney.

Assets. All of the real and personal property a person owns. Trust assets or guardianship assets are the assets transferred to the trustee or guardian.

Beneficiary. The person for whose benefit assets are held by an executor, guardian, trustee, or conservator. The person designated to receive the income of a trust estate.

Conservatee. A person under conservatorship.

Committee or conservator. Names for the guardian of an adult in some states and provinces.

Discretionary trust. A trust in which the trustee has the power to decide whether or not to give the beneficiary any of the trust assets. The trustee cannot be forced to do so.

Estate. The assets of a person who has died. The term can also be used of a trust or guardianship, as in "trust estate," in which case it means the assets of the trust or guardianship.

Executor. The person who handles the administration of a will, receiving the assets of the estate and paying the debts.

Guardian. A person who has the legal control of the affairs of another person who is incompetent. Can be guardian of the estate, guardian of the person, or both.

Guardian ad litem. A guardian appointed to represent a person in a legal action even though this guardian has no control over the person's daily life.

Informed consent. That consent which is given by a legally competent person in possession of all facts necessary for a reasonably prudent person to make a decision.

Intestate. Dying without a valid will.

Living trust. A trust that takes effect during the life of the trustor.

Mandatory. In trust language, something which the trustee must do and which can be forced by a court if the trustee fails to perform it.

Nominate. To suggest persons for the jobs of guardian, executor, conservator, or trustee. Usually done in a will.

Power of attorney. A document by which one person appoints another person to act on his or her behalf.

Principal. The person who appoints another person to act as an agent on his or her behalf, as in power of attorney.

Settlor. Same as trustor.

Successor. The person who takes over a job after another has stopped doing it, such as a successor guardian.

Testamentary trust. A trust created in a will that takes effect upon the death of the trustor.

Testate. Dying with a will.

Testator. The person making a will.

Trust. A legal entity created when one person gives another person property to manage for the giver for the benefit of the beneficiary. Usually thought of as being created in a written document setting out the terms of the trust.

Trustee. The person holding and managing the assets of a trust.

Trustor. The person giving property to a trustee to manage on the trustor's behalf for the benefit of a beneficiary.

Will. A document signed by a person, by which the person gives instructions relating to the disposition of his or her assets after death and appoints those persons who will administer the estate, including guardians, conservators, executors, and trustees.

8

Future planning checklist

Now that you've read about wills, trusts, and guardianships, you can begin specific preparations for your estate planning. The following checklist is designed to help you organize your thoughts and obtain necessary information before meeting with your attorney or other consultant.

Although gathering this information is important, going to your attorney is more so. Your attorney can get the information from you without any preparation on your part, but it will take longer. If you don't know how to gather the information, just go to your attorney.

Use this checklist as a guide, but don't let it intimidate you. The term "child" used in this checklist is intended to include family members of any age who have a disability or are dependent. Please feel free to make photocopies of the checklist.

1. Think about and discuss the following issues with your spouse:
    - ☐ Do we want to provide any funds for our dependent child through our estate?
    - ☐ Do our other children want to be involved in the permanent care of their sibling who has a disability?
    - ☐ How much of our estate do we want to devote to our child's needs?
    - ☐ Do we want to use a discretionary trust?

☐ Do we want our congregation to work with us in the supportive care plan? If not, how do we provide for continuing successor trustees, advocates, and supportive care for our dependent child?

☐ If we use a trust, who do we want to receive any funds remaining in the trust when our dependent child dies?

2. Think about and discuss with your spouse and family who should be named for the following tasks:

☐ Trustee of any trust you might create for your dependent child.

☐ Alternate trustee.

☐ Guardian of the person of your dependent child, if needed in the future.

☐ Guardian for any other children who are minors.

☐ Alternate and successor guardians.

☐ A financial institution or foundation to act as co-trustee or trustee.

3. Collect and take with you the following information:

☐ Your child's current legal status.

☐ A rough idea of the value of your major items of property.

☐ A general list of your indebtedness.

☐ A list of your child's government benefits.

☐ A list of any assets owned by the child.

☐ A list of your children's birthdates.

4. Compile and take the following documents with you:

☐ A copy of your current will, if you have one.

☐ Deeds to your real estate.

☐ Guardianship or conservatorship papers, if any.

☐ Stock and bond certificates.

☐ Bank records.

☐ Insurance policies.

☐ Pension plan information.

☐ Your divorce papers, if any.

☐ This book.

9

Sample trust language

The following examples are provided for illustration of the concepts described in this book. They do not constitute legal advice and are not offered for use by persons other than licensed attorneys. Attorneys are warned that this area of the law is volatile and that local research is required before using any language provided. The authors and publisher accept no liability for damage sustained by any person or organization as a result of the use of trust language or concepts provided in this book. Your use of this language or concepts implies an agreement to indemnify the authors and publisher from any loss or expense resulting from such use. This book is provided solely to encourage life planning and to assist attorneys by suggesting possible directions their research might take. Check additional sources for sample language.

Supportive care plan successor clause

"If for any reason Trustee 1 shall fail to act or be unable to act or continue to act as trustee, I appoint Trustee 2 to act as successor trustee. If for any reason Trustee 2 shall fail to act or be unable to act or continue to act as trustee I then delegate to the Church Council (or other appropriate body) of _____ Church the power to appoint successor trustee(s) as needed. Any appointment by said Church

Council under this paragraph shall be as effective as if I had made such appointment in this paragraph."

This language can be modified for the local situation and also used for guardians, executors, and conservators. This clause should only be used by persons participating in the supportive care plan. Attorneys should check with their local court as well as doing local research to determine the acceptability of this plan in their area.

Discretionary powers clause

"The Trustee shall pay to or apply for the benefit of Beneficiary during Beneficiary's lifetime, such amounts from the principal and/or income of the trust, up to the whole thereof, as the Trustee in the Trustee's absolute discretion may from time to time deem necessary or advisable for the satisfaction of Beneficiary's special needs. As used in this instrument, 'special needs' refers to the requisites for maintaining the beneficiary's good health, safety and welfare when, in the Trustee's absolute discretion, such requisites are not being provided by any governmental agency or entity. 'Special needs' shall include but not be limited to: medical and dental expenses; clothing and equipment; programs of training, education and treatment; and essential dietary needs."

Spendthrift clause

"No interest in the principal or income of this trust may be anticipated, assigned, or encumbered, or shall be subject to any creditor's claim or to legal process, prior to its actual receipt by Beneficiary. Furthermore, I declare that it is my intent that because this trust is to be conserved and maintained for the special needs of the Beneficiary, no part of the corpus, neither principal nor undistributed income, shall be subject to the claims of voluntary or involuntary creditors for the provision of care and services, including residential care, by any public entity, office, department or agency, including any governmental agency or entity of the United States of America, Canada, or any state or province of either, or any other governmental entity."

Intent to receive government benefits

"I declare it to be my intent, as expressed herein, that because Beneficiary is impaired so as to be incapable of full self-support, the Trustee shall, in the exercise of Trustee's discretion and duty, seek support and maintenance for Beneficiary from all available public sources. In making distributions under this trust, Trustee is to consider all public sources of income to Beneficiary and their limitations."

No replacement of public benefits

"It is further my intention that no part of the corpus of the trust herein shall be used to supplant or replace public assistance benefits to which persons with impairments similar to those of Beneficiary are entitled. No part of the trust estate shall be included in any calculation of eligibility for public benefits of Beneficiary. Trustee is authorized to defend at the expense of the trust against any attempt by any public entity to defeat the provisions of this trust for purposes of using trust assets to supplant public benefits."

Poison pill clause

"Notwithstanding anything to the contrary contained in other provisions of this trust, in the event Trustee determines in Trustee's absolute discretion that Trustee's discretionary right to use assets of the trust for the benefit of the Beneficiary has the effect of rendering the Beneficiary ineligible for public benefits, the Trustee is hereby authorized, but not required, in the Trustee's absolute discretion, to distribute all assets held in trust to (charity) and to terminate this trust. In determining whether or not the Beneficiary is being denied public benefits on the basis of the existence of the Trustee's discretionary right to use assets of the trust for the benefit of Beneficiary I hereby authorize Trustee to undertake, at the expense of the trust, such administrative and/or judicial actions as are necessary in Trustee's discretion to make such determination and to protect the right of Beneficiary to such benefits."

10

Notes to attorneys

.

The concept of a discretionary spendthrift trust has become widespread in recent years. Many states have tested the instruments and accepted them. It is relatively simple to determine whether your state has done so. Just check with the appropriate advocacy office.

Key items are absolute discretion of the trustee and clear intent that only supplemental assistance is wanted by the trustor. Minnesota lawyers must check Minnesota Statutes 501B.89. We have not done a search of the statutes of every state and province. The likelihood is that your jurisdiction has statutes affecting special needs trusts.

Some planners prefer guardianship for both asset management and personal management. Depending upon the degree of disability, guardianship of the person may or may not be necessary. The problem with guardianship of the estate as opposed to a trust is the denial of public benefits. Where the dependent person has substantial assets, this may not be an issue.

The expectation is that the trust for a dependent person will not be funded at a level that would provide full support. Determination of the amount that is reasonable will be difficult in some cases. A charitable remainder beneficiary is suggested to avoid conflict of interest among siblings, which would be to the dependent person's detriment.

If you have not reviewed the book, *Supportive Care in the Congregation*, please do so. You may find its suggestions for handling the successor trustee and guardian problem helpful. It may also be the way to avoid guardianship of the person.

There are many cases applying to this subject in all jurisdictions. The American Bar Association Probate and Trust Committee on Special Problems of the Aged and Disabled Persons is one resource. For Canadians, the Law Society of Manitoba, 1400-155 Carlton Street, Winnipeg, MB R3C 3H8 has published the helpful book, *Estate Planning for Beneficiaries with Special Needs*. One readily accessible article on government access to trusts of incompetent persons is found at 92 ALR 2d 838.

11

For additional information

Organizations

Major metropolitan areas are likely to have a legal office devoted to the concerns of people with disabilities, including mental illness. Individual states or provinces may have planning councils and offices of disabilities or mental illness, which may be another local source of estate planning materials.

The National PLAN Alliance (Planned Lifetime Assistance Network) is a national organization focusing on estate and life planning in the U.S. Members of this organization are independent, not-for-profit programs that provide care planning services to parents who wish to continue the care they currently provide into the future when they are no longer able or available to provide such care to their adult children with disabilities. Three key services offered are 1) developing a future care plan, 2) helping parents establish the necessary resources to fund the plan, and 3) identifying the persons and or programs responsible for carrying out the plan.

National PLAN Alliance
Email: npa@nycap.rr.com
Phone: (518) 587-3372
Website: www.nationalplanalliance.org

Many service organizations produce materials designed to assist estate planners. Specialized materials for families with dependent adult members are also available. The following organizations have branches in many states or provinces and may have local advocacy groups in your community:

The Arc
1660 L Street, NW, Suite 301
Washington, DC 20036
Phone: (202) 534-3700; (800) 433-5255
Website: www.thearc.org

National Alliance on Mental Illness (NAMI)
3803 N. Fairfax Dr., Ste. 100
Arlington, VA 22203
Phone: (703) 524-7600; (888) 999-6264
Website: www.nami.org

Canadian Association for Community Living
Kinsmen Building, York University
4700 Keele Street
Toronto, Ontario, Canada M3J 1P3
Phone: (416) 661-9611
Website: www.cacl.ca

Planned Lifetime Advocacy Network
#260- 3665 Kingsway
Vancouver, BC, Canada V5R 5W2
Phone (604) 439-9566
Website: www.plan.ca

Denominational resources

Anabaptist/Mennonite

Anabaptist Disabilities Network (ADNet)
PO Box 959
Goshen, IN 46527-0959
Phone: (877) 214-9838; (574) 535-7053
Websites: www.adnetonline.org

Mennonite Foundation, a division of Everence Financial
1110 North Main Street
P.O. Box 483
Goshen, IN 46527
Phone: (800) 348-7468; (574) 533-9511
Website: www.everence.org
(Ask about regional representatives with expertise in estate planning)

MHS Alliance (Mennonite Health Services)
234 South Main Street, Suite I
Goshen, Indiana 46526
Phone: (800) 611-4007; (574) 534-9689
Website: www.mhsonline.org
(Regional mental health centers and disability service providers)

Baptist

American Baptist Home Mission Society Disabilities Ministries
P.O. Box 851
Valley Forge, PA 19482-0851
Phone: (800) ABC-3USA, ext. 2394
Website: www.nationalministries.org/disability_ministries

American Baptist Homes and Caring Ministries
P.O. Box 851
Valley Forge, PA 19482-0851
Phone (800) ABC-3USA, ext. 2430
Website: www.abhcm.org

North American Mission Board, Southern Baptist Convention
Disabilities Awareness
4200 North Point Parkway
Alpharetta, Georgia 30022-4176
Phone: (800) 634-2462; (770) 410-6000
Website: www.namb.net/disabilities

Lifeway Christian Resources: Special Needs Ministry
One LifeWay Plaza
Nashville, TN 37234
Phone: (615) 251-2000
Website: www.lifeway.com/specialneeds

Catholic

National Apostolate for Inclusion Ministry
P.O. Box 218
Riverdale, MD 20738-0218
Phone: (301) 699-9500; (800) 736-1280
Website: www.nafim.org

National Catholic Partnership on Disability
415 Michigan Avenue NE
Suite 95
Washington, DC 20017-4501
Phone: (202) 529-2933; TTY: 202-529-2934
Website: www.ncpd.org

Christian Reformed

Christian Reformed Church Disability Concerns
2850 Kalamazoo Avenue, S.E.
Grand Rapids, MI 49560
Phone: (616) 224-0844
Website: www.crcna.org/disability

Church of the Brethren

Church of the Brethren Disabilities Ministry
1451 Dundee Avenue
Elgin, IL 60120-1674
Phone: (800) 323-8039; (847) 742-5100, ext. 304
Website: www.brethren.org/disabilities

Episcopal

Episcopal Disability Network
3024 E. Minnehaha Parkway
Minneapolis, MN 55406
Phone: (888) 738-3636, (612) 729-4322
Website: www.disability99.org

Episcopal Mental Illness Network
3604 Oakwood Rd.
Little Rock, AR 72202-1910
Phone: (501) 831-7321
Website: www.eminnews.com

Evangelical Covenant Church

Evangelical Covenant Church Disability Ministries
8083 W. Higgins Road
Chicago, IL 60631
Phone: (773) 784-3000
Website: www.covchurch.org/justice/disability

Lutheran

Evangelical Lutheran Church in America Disability Ministries
8765 West Higgins Road
Chicago, IL 60631-4101
Phone: (800) 638-3522, ext. 2692; (773) 380-2692
Website: www.elca.org/disability

Lutheran Church Missouri Synod
World Relief and Human Care: Disability Ministry
1333 S. Kirkwood Road
St. Louis, MO 63122
Phone: (800) 248-1930, ext. 1380 or 1381
Website: www.lcms.org/disability

Bethesda Lutheran Communities, Inc.
600 Hoffmann Drive
Watertown, WI 53094
Phone: (800) 369.4636; (920) 261-3050
Website: www.bethesdalutherancommunities.org

Thrivent Financial for Lutherans
Appleton Office:
4321 N Ballard Road, Appleton, WI 54919-0001
Minneapolis Office:
625 Fourth Avenue S, Minneapolis, MN 55415-1624
Phone: (800) 847-4836
Website: www.thrivent.com

Mennonite – see Anabaptist

Presbyterian

Presbyterians for Disability Concerns
100 Witherspoon Street
Louisville, KY 40202-1396
Phone: (888) 728-7228, ext. 5800
Website: www.pcusa.org/phewa/pdc

Reformed Church in America

Reformed Church in America Disability Concerns
4500 60th Street, SE
Grand Rapids, MI 49512-9670
Phone: (616) 698-7071
Website: www.rca.org/disability

Seventh-day Adventist

North American Division of Seventh-day Adventists Commission for People with Disabilities
12501 Old Columbia Pike
Silver Spring, MD 20904-6600
Phone: (585) 329-9295
Website: www.nadadventist.org/disability

Unitarian Universalist

Unitarian Universalist Association Congregational Life Staff Group
25 Beacon Street
Boston, MA 02108
Phone: (617) 742-2100
Website: www.uua.org/leaders/idbm/accessibility

United Church of Christ

United Church of Christ Disabilities Ministry
700 Prospect Avenue
Cleveland, Ohio 44115
Phone: (216) 736-3845; (866) 822-8224 ext. 3845
Website: www.uccdm.org

United Church of Christ Mental Illness Network
414 E. Pleasant Avenue
Sandwich, IL 60548
Phone (866) 822-8224 ext. 3845
Website: www.min-ucc.org

United Methodist

United Methodist Task Force on Disability Ministries
UMCOR Health
General Board of Global Ministries
475 Riverside Drive, Room 330
New York, NY 10115
Phone: (212) 870-3871
Website: www.umdisabilityministries.org

Interfaith resources

American Association of People with Disabilities (AAPD)
Interfaith Initiative
1629 K Street NW, Suite 905
Washington, DC 20006
Phone: (800) 840-8844; (202) 521-4311
Website: www.aapd.com

Elizabeth M. Boggs Center
on Developmental Disabilities
Community and Congregational Supports
UMDNJ
P.O. Box 2688
New Brunswick, NJ 08903-2688
Phone: (732) 235-9304
Website: www.rwjms.umdnj.edu/boggscenter

Mental Health Ministries
6707 Monte Verde Drive
San Diego, CA 92119
Website: www.mentalhealthministries.net

Pathways to Promise
Ministry and Mental Illness
5400 Arsenal Street
St. Louis, MO 63139
Phone: (314) 877-6489
Website: www.pathways2promise.org

12

Recommended reading

A Good Life: For You and Your Relative with a Disability (2004). Al Etmanski. Planned Lifetime Advocacy Network. Order from PLAN, (604) 439-9566, www.plan.ca.

A Family Handbook on Future Planning (2003). Sharon Davis, Ph.D., ed. The Arc of the United States and Rehabilitation Research and Training Center on Aging with Developmental Disabilities, Department of Disability and Human Development, College of Applied Health Sciences, University of Illinois at Chicago. Available online at internet.dscc.uic.edu/forms/psu/Future_Planning_Family_Handbook_2003.pdf.

Financial Planning: Special Needs Trusts (2005). Kristen Lewis Denzinger. *GP Solo Law Trends & News* Vol.1 (2), n.p. Available online from the American Bar Association, www.abanet.org, at www.abanet.org/genpractice/newsletter/lawtrends/0501/estate/financialplanning.html.

Life Planning for Adults With Developmental Disabilities: A Guide for Parents And Family Members (2007). Judith Greenbaum. New Harbinger Publications.

Managing a Special Needs Trust: A Guide for Trustees (2010).
Barbara D. Jackins, et al. DisAbilities Books. Order from
DisAbilities Books, 33 Pond Avenue #807, Brookline, MA
02445; phone: (617) 879-0397; www.disabilitiesbooks.com.

*Parenting an Adult with Disabilities or Special Needs: Everything
You Need to Know to Plan for and Protect Your Child's Future*
(2009). Peggy Lou Morgan. Amacom.

*Planning for the Future: Providing a Meaningful Life for a Child
with a Disability after Your Death* (6th edition, 2006). L.
Mark Russell and Arnold E Grant. Palatine, Ill.: Planning
for the Future. Order from L. Mark Russell, 86 W. King
Henry Ct., Palatine, IL 60067; phone 847-991-7451;
www.lmarkrussell.com.

*Safe and Secure: Six Steps to Creating a Good Life for People with
Disabilities* (2009). Al Etmanski, Jack Collins and Vickie
Cammack. Planned Lifetime Advocacy Network. Order
from PLAN, (604) 439-9566, www.plan.ca.

*Supportive Care in the Congregation: Providing a Congregational
Network of Care for Persons with Significant Disabilities*
(rev. ed., 2011). Dean Preheim-Bartel, Aldred H. Neufeldt,
Paul D. Leichty, and Christine J. Guth. Order from
Anabaptist Disabilities Network, P.O. Box 959, Goshen, IN
46527; (574) 535-7053, www.adnetonline.org.

About the contributors

Many people over a span of three decades have contributed toward the development of this resource for families.

A task force on life planning and guardianship formed in the early 1980s by Mennonite Developmental Disability Services created an outline that served as a guide for developing the first edition of this book, published in 1987 by Mennonite Central Committee.

Dean Preheim-Bartel, former Director of Mennonite Developmental Disability Services, served as consultant and editor for the first edition. Mitchell Kingsley did the original background research for this book in the midst of finishing law school and preparing for his bar exam.

Duane Ruth-Heffelbower, attorney at law practicing in California, wrote the original manuscript and reviewed the manuscript for subsequent editions. He was serving as Developmental Disabilities Services Coordinator for West Coast Mennonite Central Committee while writing the first edition.

Sheila Stopher Yoder, who served as MMA (Mennonite Mutual Aid, now Everence) Disabilities Program coordinator, and Art McFarlane, editor at MMA, prepared the second revised edition, published by MMA in 1996.

Christine Guth, as Program Associate for Anabaptist Disabilities Network, rewrote sections, updated the resources, added Carlos's story, and prepared the third edition for publication in 2011.

Paul Leichty, as Executive Director for Anabaptist Disabilities Network kept alive the vision that had inspired the original book: a vision of congregations as communities of inclusion and support for persons with disabilities and their families. His imagination and oversight made possible the updating and republication of this book in 2011, along with its companion book, *Supportive Care in the Congregation*.

Index

232894LV00001B/7/P

9 780836 195651